The Word Became Flesh

A Christmas Drama

Shirley Wickland

CSS Publishing Company, Inc., Lima, Ohio

THE WORD BECAME FLESH

Reprinted 2002

For more information about CSS Publishing Company resources, visit our website at www.csspub.com or e-mail us at custserv@csspub.com or call (800) 241-4056.

ISBN 978-0-7880-1286-0   PRINTED IN U.S.A.

*Lovingly dedicated to
my parents,
Anton and Dorothy Wickland,
and to my children,
Anthony,
Sumathy,
Daniel and Anne*

Preface

The Word Became Flesh tells the story of Jesus Christ, from creation to present day. Scriptures from throughout the Bible weave together the presence and meaning of God's Word, Jesus Christ, throughout history. Often, at Christmas we focus only on the birth of Jesus as God's incredible gift of love. This drama is unique in that it highlights Jesus' birth as part of the greater picture of Jesus throughout history: in creation, in the words of the prophets, in the cross, in the resurrection, and in our world today.

I wrote this play because, as a Sunday school teacher, I wanted to present a Christmas drama that would highlight Holy Scriptures and enable participants to learn and understand them. I also wanted to weave the Christmas story into an overall view of the Bible and the living faith that we experience today. *The Word Became Flesh* provides drama that is biblically sound, educational, and thought-provoking.

Production Notes

This program is a formal Christmas nativity pageant. It can be presented by children, by adults, or by both children and adults together. The production is easily staged with a few props (manger, cross, scrolls, shepherd staffs). The drama is most effective when the readers surround the audience, with voices following each other from the front, sides, and back. Portable lights will be needed for the readers during the times of darkness. Lighting should be used to direct attention from the manger scene, to the cross, and back during the presentation.

Traditional costumes (robes and head coverings) may be used for Mary, Joseph, the shepherds, the three wise men, and the prophets. Angels can be dressed in white robes or dresses with tinsel garland halos laid on their heads.

A church sanctuary is an ideal setting for this drama, but any large room could be used.

A separate choir, duet, or soloist could provide the singing, or the cast and/or readers could be the choir.

If a small number of people are available, prophets can double as shepherds, readers can read more than one part, and fewer angels could be included in the Heavenly Host, bringing the minimum cast size to 14. For larger groups, 24 parts are available, with potential for even more when a separate choir is used.

Scripture is from the New Revised Standard Version and the King James Version (noted).

The Word Became Flesh

Processional: "There's A Song In The Air" by Josiah G. Holland or "Joyful, Joyful We Adore Thee" by Henry Van Dyke

Lights down, almost dark. A manger is positioned in the center of the stage. A large cross is hanging above and slightly behind it.

Reader 1: "In the beginning God created the heavens and the earth." (Genesis 1:1)

Reader 2: "In the beginning was the Word, and the Word was with God, and the Word was God." (John 1:1)

Reader 3: "In the beginning God created the heavens and the earth." (Genesis 1:1)

Reader 4: "And God said, 'Let there be light.' " (Genesis 1:3)

Lights go on.

Reader 5: "Let there be a dome in the midst of the waters, and let it separate the waters from the waters." (Genesis 1:6)

Reader 6: "Let the waters under the sky be gathered together into one place, and let the dry land appear." (Genesis 1:9)

Reader 1: "Let there be lights in the dome of the sky to separate the day from the night." (Genesis 1:14)

Reader 2: "Let the waters bring forth swarms of living creatures, and let the birds fly above the earth across the dome of the sky." (Genesis 1:20)

Reader 3: "Let the earth bring forth living creatures of every kind ... And let us make humankind in our image, according to our likeness; and let them have dominion over the fish of the sea, and over the birds of the air, and over the cattle, and over all the wild animals of the earth, and over every creeping thing that creeps on the earth." (Genesis 1:24, 26) ... "So God created humankind in God's image, male and female they were created ... And God saw everything that had been made, and indeed, it was very good." (Genesis 1:27, 31)

Reader 4: "Thus the heavens and earth were finished." (Genesis 2:1)

Reader 5: "In the beginning was the Word, and the Word was with God, and the Word was God." (John 1:1) ... "And the Word became flesh and lived among us." (John 1:14) And the Word was the Son of God, Jesus Christ our Lord.

Reader 6: Just as our words are a reflection of our inner beings, so Jesus as the Word is for us a reflection of God, the "exact imprint of God's very being." (Hebrews 1:3)

Prophets enter and stand center stage (in front of the manger), each holding and unrolling a scroll.

Reader 1: And the people of God grew in numbers, and prophets arose, saying:

Prophet 1: "The Lord will give you a sign. Look, the young woman is with child and shall bear a son and shall name him Immanuel." (Isaiah 7:14)

Prophet 2: "But you, O Bethlehem ... from you shall come forth for me one who is to rule in Israel, whose origin is from old, from ancient days ... And he shall stand and feed his flock in the strength of the Lord, in the majesty of the name of the Lord his God. And they shall live secure, for now he shall be great to the ends of the earth; and he shall be the one of peace." (Micah 5:2-5)

Prophet 3: "A voice cries out: 'In the wilderness prepare the way of the Lord, make straight in the desert a highway for our God. Every valley shall be lifted up, and every mountain and hill be made low; the uneven ground shall become level, and the rough places a plain. Then the glory of the Lord shall be revealed, and all people shall see it together, for the mouth of the Lord has spoken.' " (Isaiah 40:3-5)

Prophet 1: "A shoot shall come out from the stump of Jesse, and a branch shall grow out of his roots. The spirit of the Lord shall rest upon him, the spirit of wisdom and understanding, the spirit of counsel and might, the spirit of knowledge and the fear of the Lord. His delight shall be in the fear of the Lord. He shall not judge by what his eyes see, or decide by what his ears hear; but with righteousness he shall judge the poor, and decide with equity for the meek of the earth ... Righteousness shall be the belt around his waist, and faithfulness the belt around his loins. The wolf shall live with the lamb, the leopard shall lie down with the kid, the calf and the lion and the fatling together, and a little child shall lead them." (Isaiah 11:1-6)

Prophet 2: "I saw one like a human being coming with the clouds of heaven. And he came to the Ancient One and was presented before him. To him was given dominion and glory and kingship, that all peoples, nations, and languages should serve him. His dominion is an everlasting dominion that shall not pass away, and his kingship is one that shall never be destroyed." (Daniel 7:13-14)

Prophet 3: "But this is the covenant that I will make with the House of Israel after those days, says the Lord: I will put my law within them, and I will write it on their hearts; I will be their God, and they shall be my people. No longer shall they teach one another, or say to each other, 'Know the Lord,' for they shall all know me, from the least of them to the greatest, says the Lord; for I will forgive their iniquity, and remember their sin no more." (Jeremiah 31:33-34)

Prophets exit.

11

Choir: "He Is Born" — verse 1 (French carol, harmony by Carlton R. Young)

Gabriel and Mary enter and stand center stage, in front of the manger.

Reader 2: Many years later, after all the prophecies, the angel Gabriel appeared to a young woman named Mary, saying:

Gabriel: "Greetings, favored one! The Lord is with you." (Luke 1:28) ... "Do not be afraid, Mary, for you have found favor with God. And now, you will conceive in your womb and bear a son, and you will name him Jesus. He will be great, and will be called the Son of the Most High, and the Lord God will give him the throne of his ancestor David. He will reign over the house of Jacob forever, and of his kingdom there will be no end." (Luke 1:30-33)

Mary: "Here am I, the servant of the Lord; let it be with me according to your word." (Luke 1:38)

Gabriel moves to stand behind manger. Mary faces congregation and looks up.

Mary: "My soul magnifies the Lord, and my spirit rejoices in God, my Savior,
for God has looked with favor on the lowliness of this servant.
Surely, from now on all generations will call me blessed;
For the Mighty One has done great things for me, and holy is God's name.
God's mercy is for those who fear God from generation to generation.
God has shown great strength and has scattered the proud in the thoughts of their hearts.
God has brought down the powerful from their thrones, and lifted up the lowly;
God has filled the hungry with good things, and sent the rich away empty.

12

God has helped Israel, in remembrance and mercy,
according to the promises made to our ancestors, to Abraham and
Sarah, and to their descendants forever." (Luke 1:47-55)

*Joseph and angels enter. Mary, Joseph, and Gabriel gather around
manger. All angels (Heavenly Host) stand behind them.*

Choir: "He Is Born" — verse 2

Reader 3: "And it came to pass in those days, that there went out
a decree from Caesar Augustus, that all the world should be taxed
... And all went to be taxed, every one into his own city. And Joseph also went up from Galilee, out of the city of Nazareth, into
Judea, unto the city of David called Bethlehem, because he was of
the house and lineage of David, to be taxed with Mary, his espoused wife, being great with child. And so it was, that, while they
were there, the days were accomplished that she should be delivered. And she brought forth her firstborn son, and wrapped him in
swaddling clothes and laid him in a manger, because there was no
room for them in the inn. *(Shepherds enter left stage.)* And there
were in the same country shepherds abiding in the field, keeping
watch over their flock by night. And lo, the angel of the Lord came
upon them, and the glory of the Lord shone round them, and they
were sore afraid. And the angel said unto them," (Luke 2:1-10 KJV)

Lead Angel: "Fear not, for behold, I bring you good tidings of
great joy, which shall be to all people. For unto you is born this day
in the city of David a Savior, which is Christ the Lord. And this
shall be a sign unto you; You shall find the babe wrapped in swaddling clothes, lying in a manger." (Luke 2:10-12 KJV)

Reader 4: "And suddenly there was with the angel a multitude of
the heavenly host praising God, and saying," (Luke 2:13 KJV)

All angels (the Heavenly Host): "Glory to God in the highest,
and on earth, peace and good will toward all." (Luke 2:14 KJV)

Reader 5: "And it came to pass, as the angels were gone away from them into heaven, the shepherds said one to another," (Luke 2:15a KJV)

Lead Shepherd: "Let us now go even unto Bethlehem, and see this thing which is come to pass, which the Lord hath made known to us." (Luke 2:15b KJV)

Shepherds move to left side of nativity scene and kneel.

Reader 6: "And they came with haste, and found Mary and Joseph, and the babe lying in a manger. And when they had seen it, they made known abroad the saying which was told them concerning this child. And all that heard it wondered at those things which were told them by the shepherds. But Mary kept all these things and pondered them in her heart." (Luke 2:16-19 KJV)

Wise men enter, present gifts, and kneel at the right of the nativity scene during this reading.

Reader 1: "Behold, there came wise men from the east," (Matthew 2:1b KJV) "and lo, the star, which they saw in the east, went before them, till it came and stood over where the young child was. When they saw the star they rejoiced with exceeding great joy. And when they came ... they saw the young child with Mary, his mother, and fell down and worshiped him: and when they had opened their treasures, they presented unto him gifts of gold and frankincense and myrrh." (Matthew 2:9b-11 KJV)

Choir: "He Is Born" — verse 3

Reader 2: "For unto us a child is born, unto us a son is given, and the government shall be upon his shoulder, and his name shall be called Wonderful, Counselor, Almighty God, the everlasting Father, the Prince of Peace." (Isaiah 9:6 KJV)

Reader 3: "And the boy Jesus increased in wisdom and in years, and in divine and human favor." (Luke 2:52)

Reader 4: "And the Word became flesh and lived among us, and we have seen his glory." (John 1:14)

Reader 5: And Jesus became a great teacher. Jesus taught our world how to love with words like these:

Reader 6: "You shall love the Lord your God with all your heart, and with all your soul, and with all your mind ... and you shall love your neighbor as yourself." (Matthew 22:37-39)

Reader 1: "Blessed are the poor in spirit: for theirs is the kingdom of heaven.
Blessed are they that mourn: for they shall be comforted.
Blessed are the meek: for they shall inherit the earth.
Blessed are they which do hunger and thirst after righteousness: for they shall be filled.
Blessed are the merciful: for they shall obtain mercy.
Blessed are the pure in heart: for they shall see God.
Blessed are the peacemakers: for they shall be called children of God.
Blessed are they which are persecuted for righteousness' sake: for theirs is the kingdom of heaven.
Blessed are you when people revile you and persecute you and utter all kinds of evil against you falsely for my sake. Rejoice and be exceeding glad, for great is your reward in heaven: for so persecuted they the prophets which were before you." (Matthew 5:3-12 KJV)

Reader 2: "Whoever welcomes one such child in my name welcomes me, and whoever welcomes me welcomes the one who sent me; for the least among all of you is the greatest." (Luke 9:48)

Reader 3: "Come, you that are blessed by the Creator, inherit the kingdom prepared for you from the foundation of the world; for I was hungry and you gave me food, I was thirsty and you gave me something to drink, I was a stranger and you welcomed me, I was naked and you gave me clothing, I was sick and you took care of me, I was in prison and you visited me." (Matthew 25:34a-36) ... "Truly, I tell you, just as you did it to one of the least of these who are members of my family, you did it to me." (Matthew 25:40)

Reader 4: "By this, everyone will know that you are my disciples, if you have love for one another." (John 13:35)

Reader 5: Jesus taught the people and healed the sick and fed the hungry and showed an entire world how to love one another.

Reader 6: And finally Jesus said, "I am the good shepherd. The good shepherd lays down his life for the sheep." (John 10:11)

Reader 1: "For God so loved the world, that God gave his only son, that whosoever believes should not perish, but have eternal life." (John 3:16, paraphrased)

Lights move from nativity scene to cross above it.

Reader 2: And Jesus was crucified on a cross, and the inscription above his head read "King of the Jews."

All lights go out.

Reader 3: "It was now about noon, and darkness came over the whole land until three in the afternoon, while the sun's light failed; and the curtain of the Temple was torn in two. Then Jesus, crying in a loud voice said, 'Father, into your hands I commend my spirit.'" (Luke 23:44-46)

Reader 4: "For God so loved the world, that God gave his only son, that whosoever believes should not perish, but have eternal life." (John 3:16)

Reader 5: And the mystery of the cross is that God loves us,

Reader 6: ... that God forgives us,

Reader 1: ... that God suffers with us,

Reader 2: ... that God calls us to love each other,

Reader 3: ... and that even death cannot separate us from the absolute, unconditional love of God, through God's own Word, Jesus Christ.

Lights back on cross; the rest of the room is dark.

Reader 4: "And on the third day he rose ... and ascended into heaven, and is seated at the right hand of God and will come again to judge the living and the dead." (Apostles' Creed)

Reader 5: "Beloved, let us love one another, because love is from God; everyone who loves is born of God and knows God. Whoever does not love does not know God, for God is love. God's love was revealed among us in this way: God's only son was sent into the world so that we might live through him. In this is love, not that we loved God but that God loved us and sent Jesus to be the atoning sacrifice for our sins. Beloved, since God loved us so much, we also ought to love one another. If we love one another, God lives in us, and God's love is perfected in us." (1 John 4:7-12)

Reader 6: "Listen, I will tell you a mystery! We will not all die, but we will all be changed, in a moment, in the twinkling of an eye, at the last trumpet ... Death has been swallowed up in victory. O death, where is your victory? O death, where is your sting? The sting of death is sin, and the power of sin is the law. But thanks be to God, who gives us the victory through our Lord Jesus Christ." (1 Corinthians 15:51-57)

Reader 1: "Let the same mind be in you that was in Christ Jesus, who, though he was in the form of God, did not regard equality with God as something to be exploited, but emptied himself, taking the form of a slave, being born in human likeness. And being found in human form, he humbled himself and became obedient to the point of death, even death on a cross. Therefore God also highly exalted him and gave him the name that is above every name, so that at the name of Jesus every knee should bend, in heaven and on earth and under the earth, and every tongue should confess that Jesus Christ is Lord, to the glory of God the Creator." (Philippians 2:5-11)

Reader 2: "For God so loved the world, that God gave his only son, that whosoever believes should not perish, but have eternal life." (John 3:16)

Lights back on nativity scene and cross.

Choir: "He Lives" by Alfred H. Ackley

Reader 3: And now each year, at Christmas, we remember a baby born in a Bethlehem stable.

Reader 4: A baby who was long awaited and foretold by the prophets.

Reader 5: A baby who is the reflection of God's love for us, the "exact imprint of God's very being." (Hebrews 1:3)

Reader 6: A baby who was with God in the beginning, who is with God into eternity, and who is with us at this very moment.

Reader 1: Each year we remember the manger and we remember the cross.

Reader 2: And each year we rejoice and celebrate the birth of our Lord, the King of kings, the Prince of Peace.

Reader 3: "Glory to God in the highest and on earth, peace, and good will to all." (Luke 2:14 KJV)

Reader 4: "For unto us a child is born, unto us a son is given, and the government shall be upon his shoulder, and his name shall be called,

Reader 5: Wonderful, Counselor,

Reader 6: Almighty God,

Reader 1: the everlasting Father,

Reader 2: the Prince of Peace." (Isaiah 9:6 KJV)

All: Hallelujah!

Recessional: "Joy To The World" by Isaac Watts

Cast exits down center or side aisles during the last verse of this song.